GW01179366

Eleanor's Home Baking

Simply Delicious Baking Recipes

from a Cornwall Kitchen

Eleanor Knowles

Copyright © 2016, Eleanor Knowles

All rights reserved

ISBN-13: 978-1518691362

ISBN-10: 1518691366

This book is for everyone and anyone who would rather eat homemade goodies than shop-bought ones. Baking isn't difficult, but it can be time-consuming...
...and it's definitely addictive!

Eleanor's Home Baking

Simply Delicious Recipes from a Cornwall Kitchen

Contents

Acknowledgements

Never-ending thanks to my Mum, Libby, who taught me to cook properly and answered my endless questions. Over the years I've added my own tricks and twists to old favourites and family specials, developing new recipes along the way. It's been great fun – even doing the nerve-wracking one-off birthday cakes – and I'm still learning about what works and what doesn't. So I'd love to share these tips with you.

Also huge thanks to Cofro in Mevagissey for placing the first order from Eleanor's Home Baking back in 2009. My one-woman baking business has since grown to supply a loyal band of regular customers, businesses and individuals. Thank you all.

1   Getting Started

Baking is a bit like alchemy. Bring the right ingredients together with the right instructions and some heat, and – *abracadabra!* – a golden sponge appears.

Baking can be entertainment too, just look at all the TV shows on the subject. We can't get enough of it, and sales of ready made cakes are soaring. Britain is a nation famed for its afternoon tea, yet lots of us don't bake at all. It's about time to change that, surely?

With wafts of sweet spices rising from the oven and the warm temptations of freshly baked cakes and quiches filling the air, the kitchen suddenly seems like a great place to spend some time. I've loved cooking since I was tall enough to see over the worktop, kneading pastry trimmings into grey shiny blobs and 'helping Mummy' in the kitchen.

Baking is great fun, and a wonderful way to de-stress, so I hope you will be brave – put on a (clean) apron and grab your wooden spoon – and enjoy having a go. Never worry about the end result, trust me, there is always someone around who will want to eat it!

Fortunately you can start baking without too much kit. Weighing scales, measuring spoons, a large bowl, two sandwich tins, a bun tray and a couple of spatulas are all you need to get going. *Tip* – using a clear bowl makes it easier to see when the ingredients are fully mixed.

Non-stick paper liners can be very useful – no need to butter the tins – and they are available in a variety of sizes. And cocktail sticks make handy cake testers.

But the most important element of baking is the one in your oven. You have to know if your oven is doing what it says, and I strongly recommend buying an oven thermometer to check its temperature.

Though swish expensive ovens may look great, a tiny tabletop model will do the baking just as well.

A fan oven should have an even temperature on all shelves, whereas a non-fan oven is hotter nearer the heating element (usually at the top).

Any oven can be slightly hotter on one side than on the other, sometimes because it's not level. This can make one side start to brown first, especially sponge cakes for some reason, so rotate the food halfway through cooking to ensure even baking.

And some ovens do seem to cook faster than others for no apparent reason... so watch your baking carefully while it's in there. *Tip* – if the cake is making a lot of noise, it's not quite done.

2   Ingredients

This isn't rocket science. Buy the best quality ingredients you can find. That doesn't always mean the most expensive, by the way. Fresh and local will almost always be better and cheaper.

OK, I know shop-bought cakes and biscuits are far less expensive than making your own. But do they taste as good? Thought not.

I'm sure you've got your own favourte ingredients but, in case you're wondering, here are some of the ones I like because I find they give consistently good results.

Flour – freshness is everything, if it smells musty or mouldy don't use it, and NEVER use out of date flour. Own-brand flours tend to have a higher turnover than branded ones, so I use whichever flour seems to be flying off the shelves fastest.

Gluten-free flour – as above. There seems to be a lot of variation in the constituents of gluten-free fiours, but I've had better results with own-brands than branded ones. Using a self-raising type avoids the need to add separate xanthan gum to replicate the action of gluten.

Butter – local or British. I use Trewithen Cornish salted butter. (I don't use margarine, too many E-numbers.)

Milk and cream – local or British. I like Trewithen Cornish milk, cream and clotted cream.

Eggs – always free-range, ideally local and certainly British. I use St Ewe eggs or other Cornish ones.

Oils – corn oil is best for baking, as it doesn't give off a 'burned fat' smell at high temperatures. I like Mazola. For olive oil in baking recipes, I tend to use pale gold rather than extra virgin. The lovely grassiness of virgin olive oil tends to dissipate on heating, so save it for salad dressings.

Sugar – unrefined sugars are best for flavour and, for me at least, don't give such a sharp sugar rush. I use Billington's or other fairtrade unrefined cane sugars.

Icing sugar – ideally unrefined, but it can be difficult to find and does give a slight beige colour to icing, so you might prefer to use the white stuff. There is little difference between beet and cane sugar in the end results. Royal icing sugar is best for fancy piping.

Cocoa – I prefer Green & Black's organic cocoa powder, as it gives smoother results in the recipes here, but try UTZ certified brands too.

Dried fruit – own-brands are often better than branded ones because they have a quicker turnover. If the fruit in the packet looks plump and juicy, buy it.

Nuts – choose whichever look the best, and have the longest shelf life. Taste before you bake and discard any that seem stale or are bitter or rancid.

Vanilla – extract or paste, not essence or flavouring. I use Madagascan vanilla extract or vanilla bean paste, it's expensive but you need only a tiny amount. Keep it in the fridge once opened.

Citrus fruit – ideally unwaxed. Look for unblemished peel and fruit that feels heavy for its size.

Other flavouring extracts – don't bother. Those small bottles are usually a solution of artificial flavours in alcohol and, to my mind, give an unpleasant tang to the finished product. Use real ingredients!

3   Recipe notes

A few hints to help you get the best out of the recipes. You may have heard it all before, but here goes...

- Read the recipe through (twice) before you start, so you know you have everything you need and enough time to bake.
- Stick to metric or imperial measurements, don't mix them within a recipe.
- Weigh and measure your ingredients carefully.
- Wash all fruit and vegetables before using.

In this book...

- All spoon measures are level.
- Oven temperatures are in degrees Celsius.
- Bakes go onto the centre shelf of the oven.
- The finished articles are suitable for freezing unless stated otherwise.

Measures used here...

5ml spoon = 1 tsp = 1 teaspoon

10ml spoon = 1 dsp = 1 dessertspoon = 2 tsp

15ml spoon = 1 tbsp = 1 tablespoon = 3 tsp

568ml = 1 pint = 20 fluid ounces = 20 fluid oz

454 g = 16 oz = 1 pound = 1 lb

28 g = 1 oz

2.5 cm = 1 inch = 1 in

4   Small cakes, muffins and cupcakes

Easy to make, even easier to eat.

Light chocolate cakes

Double dark chocolate muffins

Lemon buns

Spiced fresh berry muffins

Coffee pecan cupcakes

White velvet cupcakes

Cherry cakes

Light Chocolate Cakes

Rich and light. Makes 12 cupcakes

5 oz	plain flour	140 g
2 tbsp	cocoa powder	30 ml
2 tsp	baking powder	10 ml
¼ tsp	salt	1.25 ml
2 oz	butter	55 g
1½ oz	light soft brown sugar	40 g
1	free-range egg	1
4 fluid oz	milk	115 ml
2 oz	dark chocolate drops	55 g

Preheat your oven to 200ºC (190ºC fan). Line a 12-hole cupcake or jam tart tray with 2 inch (5 cm) paper cake cases.

Melt the butter in a large pan over a low heat (or in the microwave), and allow to cool. Sift the flour, cocoa powder, baking powder and salt into a bowl.

Mix the sugar, egg and milk thoroughly into the cooled, but still molten, butter. Sift the dry ingredients once again, but straight onto the wet ones. Mix together quickly, the mixture should still look rather lumpy. Stir in the chocolate drops, and spoon the mixture into the paper cases.

Bake the muffins for about 15-18 minutes, until risen and firm to the touch. Test with a cocktail stick – it should come out clean. Cool for at least 5 minutes in the tray before transferring to a cooling rack.

Cook's notes

These little cakes are best eaten within 2 days.

Variation

Add 1 oz (30 g) chopped glacé ginger with the chocolate drops.

Double Dark Chocolate Muffins

Moist and deeply chocolatey. Makes 12 large muffins

10 oz	self-raising flour	285 g
3 tbsp	cocoa powder	45 ml
1 tsp	bicarbonate of soda	5 ml
3 oz	dark brown soft sugar	85 g
3 oz	Demerara sugar	85 g
4 fluid oz	corn oil	115 ml
½ pint	milk	285 ml
½ tsp	vanilla extract	2.5 ml
2 tbsp	golden syrup	30 ml
3½ oz	dark chocolate drops	100 g

Preheat your oven to 190ºC (180ºC fan). Line a 12-hole muffin tray with 2.5 inch (7.5 cm) paper muffin cases.

Sift the flour, cocoa powder and bicarbonate of soda into a bowl. Stir in the sugars. Add the oil, milk and vanilla extract, and mix briefly but thoroughly. Mix in the syrup. Stir in half of the chocolate drops, and spoon the mixture into the paper cups. Sprinkle over the rest of the chocolate drops.

Bake the muffins for about 18-20 minutes, until well risen and springy to the touch. Test with a cocktail stick – it should come out clean. Cool for at least 10 minutes in the tray before transferring to a cooling rack.

Cook's notes

These muffins keep well in an airtight container for 4-5 days.

Make it a little lighter

Use the Light Chocolate Cakes recipe, but make into 8 muffins instead of 12 cupcakes.

Lemon Buns

Zingy and great with yoghurt. Makes 12 buns

2	large lemons (or 3 small ones)	2
6 oz	golden caster sugar	170 g
6 oz	soft butter	170 g
8 oz	self-raising flour	225 g
1½ tsp	baking powder	7.5 ml
3 tbsp	milk	45 ml
3	free-range eggs	3
4 tbsp	lemon curd	60 ml
	icing sugar	

Preheat your oven to 180°C (170°C fan). Line a 12-hole cupcake or jam tart tray with 2 inch (5 cm) paper cake cases.

Finely grate all the zest from the lemons into a bowl. Add the caster sugar and butter. Beat together until light and fluffy. Sift over the flour and baking powder. Stir in the eggs and milk. Mix thoroughly but gently until combined.

Divide half of the mixture equally between the paper cases. Spoon 1 tsp (5 ml) of lemon curd into each case and top with the remaining sponge mixture. Bake for about 25 minutes or until golden brown, well risen and springy to the touch. Test with a cocktail stick – it should come out clean.

Meanwhile, squeeze the juice from the lemons into a measuring jug, discarding any pips. For every 1 tbsp (15 ml) of juice, add ½ tbsp (7.5 ml) of icing sugar and stir to dissolve. As soon as the buns are ready, drizzle over the syrup and allow them to cool completely in the tray.

Cook's notes

Use good quality lemon curd for the buns – or try making your own.

These buns keep well in an airtight container for 3-4 days.

Variation

For orange buns, replace the lemons with 1 large orange and reduce the caster sugar by 1 oz (30 g). Use 1 tsp (5 ml) icing sugar per 1 tbsp (15 ml) orange juice in the syrup. If you can find orange curd, then try it instead of lemon curd.

Spiced Fresh Berry Muffins

Use your favourite berries – blueberries, blackcurrants or raspberries all work well. Makes 12 large muffins

9 oz	plain flour	255 g
1 tbsp	baking powder	15 ml
¼ tsp	salt	1.25 ml
½ tsp	mixed spice	2.5 ml
3 oz	butter	85 g
2¼ oz	golden caster sugar	65 g
2	free-range eggs	2
¼ pint	milk	145 ml
7 oz	punnet of fresh berries	200 g

Preheat your oven to 190ºC (180ºC fan). Line a 12-hole muffin tray with 2.5 inch (7.5 cm) paper muffin cases.

Melt the butter in a large pan over a low heat (or in the microwave), and allow to cool. Sift the flour, baking powder, salt and mixed spice into a bowl.

Mix the sugar, egg and milk thoroughly into the cooled, but still molten, butter. Sift the dry ingredients once again, but straight onto the wet ones. Mix together gently but quickly, the mixture should still look rather lumpy. Stir in the berries, and spoon the mixture into the paper cases.

Bake the muffins for about 25 minutes, until risen and firm to the touch. Test with a cocktail stick – it should come out clean. Cool for at least 5 minutes in the tray before transferring to a ccoling rack.

Cook's notes

These muffins are good served warm, and best eaten within 2 days. Not suitable for freezing.

Make it a little lighter

Make into 18 small cupcakes instead of 12 muffins.

Coffee Pecan Cupcakes

Satisfyingly nutty. Makes 12 large cupcakes

Cakes

1-2 tbsp	instant coffee granules	15-30 ml
2 tbsp	boiling water	30 ml
10 oz	self-raising flour	285 g
1 tsp	bicarbonate of soda	5 ml
3 oz	light soft brown sugar	85 g
3 oz	Demerara sugar	85 g
4 fluid oz	corn oil	115 ml
9 fluid oz	milk	250 ml
2 tbsp	golden syrup	30 ml
2 oz	chopped pecan nuts	55 g

Icing

4 oz	soft butter	115 g
10 oz	icing sugar	285 g
1 tbsp	instant coffee granules	15 ml
1 tbsp	boiling water	15 ml
12	pecan halves	12

Preheat your oven to 190ºC (180ºC fan). Line a 12-hole muffin tray with 2.5 inch (7.5 cm) paper cases. Dissolve the coffee granules in the boiling water and set aside.

Sift the flour and bicarbonate of soda into a bowl. Stir in the sugars. Add the oil, milk and coffee liquid, and mix briefly. Mix in the syrup and chopped pecans. Spoon the mixture into the paper cups.

Bake the muffins for about 20 minutes, until well risen and springy to the touch. Test with a cocktail stick – it should come out clean. Cool for at least 10 minutes in the tray before transferring to a cooling rack.

When the cupcakes are cold, make the icing. Dissolve the coffee granules in the boiling water and set aside.

Beat the soft butter, icing sugar and coffee liquid together until light and fluffy – a mixer or a food processor is handy here. Swirl or pipe the coffee buttercream on top of the cupcakes and decorate each one with a pecan half.

Cook's notes

These cupcakes keep well in an airtight container fo⁻ 2-3 days.

Make it a little lighter

Make into 18 smaller cupcakes instead of 12. You will need 18 pecan halves for decoration.

Variation

For a nut-free version, replace the chopped pecans in the batter with golden sultanas and decorate the buttercream topping with white chocolate chips instead of pecan halves.

White Velvet Cupcakes

Light but luscious. Makes 12 cupcakes

Cakes

4 oz	golden caster sugar	110 g
2 oz	soft butter	55 g
½ tsp	vanilla extract	2.5 ml
	grated zest of 1 lemon (optional)	
1	large free-range egg	1
5 oz	self-raising flour, sifted	140 g
4¼ oz	plain or lemon low-fat yoghurt	120 g
2 tsp	lemon juice	10 ml
½ tsp	bicarbonate of soda	2.5 ml

Frosting

3½ oz	cream cheese	100 g
1¾ oz	soft butter	50 g
5¼ oz	icing sugar	150 g
¼ tsp	vanilla extract	1.25 ml

Preheat your oven to 170ºC (160ºC fan). Line a 12-hole cupcake or jam tart tray with 2 inch (5 cm) paper cake cases.

Cream the sugar, butter, vanilla extract and grated lemon zest (if using) together in a bowl until soft and light. Beat in the egg, then fold in half the flour.

Mix the yoghurt, lemon juice and bicarbonate of soda in a jug – it will foam up. Pour onto the cake batter and stir in quickly but thoroughly. Fold in the remaining flour.

Divide the batter between the paper cases, working as fast as you can so that the bubbles created by the liquid mixture don't deflate too much. Pop the tin into the oven and bake for around 20 minutes. When ready the cakes will spring back when pressed and a cocktail stick will come out clean.

Cool on a wire rack. Do not frost the cupcakes until they are completely cold.

For the frosting, mix the cream cheese, butter, icing sugar and vanilla extract together until creamy. *Tip* – be careful not to over beat the mixture or it could separate. Swirl the frosting on top of the cupcakes, but don't expect it to set firmly. Serve as soon as possible.

Cook's notes

Use 3.5 fluid oz (100 ml) of buttermilk in place of the yoghurt if you prefer.

The cupcakes are best eaten on the same day they are frosted, but they can be kept overnight in an airtight container in the fridge.

Not suitable for freezing.

Variation

For the more well-known red velvet cupcakes, add a lot (I do mean a LOT) of red gel food colour – at least 1 tbsp (15 ml) – with the egg and 2 tsp (10 ml) cocoa powder with the flour. Omit the lemon zest.

Cherry Cakes

Always popular, especially with children. Makes 12 cakes

Cakes

6 oz	golden caster sugar	170 g
6 oz	soft butter	170 g
8 oz	self-raising flour	225 g
1½ tsp	baking powder	7.5 ml
3 tbsp	milk	45 ml
3	free-range eggs	3
2 oz	glacé cherries, chopped	55 g

Icing

9 oz	icing sugar	255 g
1	lemon	1
6	glacé cherries	6

Preheat your oven to 180ºC (170ºC fan). Line a 12-hole cupcake or jam tart tray with 2 inch (5 cm) paper cake cases.

Beat the butter and caster sugar until light and fluffy. Sift over the flour and baking powder. Stir in the eggs, milk and chopped glacé cherries. Mix thoroughly but gently until combined.

Divide the mixture equally between the paper cases. Bake for 20-22 minutes until golden brown, well risen and springy to the touch. Test with a cocktail stick – it should come out clean. Cool for at least 10 minutes in the tray before transferring to a cooling rack.

For the icing, grate the lemon zest into a bowl. Add the icing sugar and mix in enough of the lemon's juice to make a thick icing. Spread over the tops of the cakes and decorate each one with half a glacé cherry.

Cook's notes

These cakes keep well in an airtight container for 2-3 days, and can be frozen without the icing and decoration.

Variation

In summer, decorate each cake with several fresh cherries instead of the glacé cherry halves. Eat the same day.

5   Traybakes, flapjacks and biscuits

Scrumptious bites with tea or coffee.

Chocolate brownies

Apricot flapjacks

Cranberry and orange squares

Fruity muesli bars

Almond biscuits

Ginger fairings

Chocolate Brownies

Rich and fudgy. Makes 12 generous brownies

3 oz	dark chocolate (50% cocoa)	85 g
3 oz	milk chocolate	85 g
3 oz	butter	85 g
3¼ oz	self-raising flour	90 g
1 oz	cocoa powder	30 g
6 oz	Demerara sugar	170 g
1 oz	raisins	30 g
3	free-range eggs	3

Preheat your oven to 180ºC (170ºC fan). Line a 9 inch (22.5 cm) square tin with non-stick foil or baking paper. *Tip* – wet the tin to help it stick.

Melt the chocolates and butter in a pan over a low heat, stir and allow to cool a little.

Sift the flour and cocoa powder into a bowl. Stir in the sugar and raisins. Add the eggs and mix well. Tip the melted chocolate and butter into the bowl and mix thoroughly. Pour the batter into the tin and spread right into the corners.

Bake the brownies for about 20-25 minutes, until the top is firm to the touch but gives a little underneath. Test with a cocktail stick – it should come out with a few damp crumbs attached.

Allow the brownies to cool completely in the tin. Lift out the whole lot in the foil or paper and cut into 12 pieces.

Cook's notes

The brownies are best eaten within 2 days, if any last that long.

Make it a little lighter

Reduce the Demerara sugar by 1 oz (30 g) and cut the brownies into 16 squares.

Variation

For a special treat, pour 1-2 tsp (5-10 ml) of dark rum or brandy over the raisins and leave until they have plumped up.

Apricot Flapjacks

Good in a lunchbox. Makes 12 flapjacks

3½ oz	golden syrup	100 g
4 oz	butter	115 g
2½ oz	Demerara sugar	70 g
3½ oz	chopped dried apricots	100 g
8 oz	porridge oats	225 g

Preheat your oven to 150ºC (140ºC fan). Line a 9 inch (22.5 cm) square or 8x10 inch (20x25 cm) roasting tin with non-stick foil or baking paper. *Tip* – wet the tin to help it stick.

Melt the syrup, butter and Demerara sugar in a pan over a low heat, stir and allow to cool a little. Add the apricots and oats and mix very well.

Tip the mixture into the tin and spread level. Bake for 35-45 minutes, turning the tin round once, or until golden brown. Mark into 12 pieces while still warm and leave to cool in the tin.

This recipe produces chewy flapjacks. For a crunchier finish, bake at 200ºC (190ºC fan) for about 20 minutes.

Cook's notes

The flapjacks keep well for a week or so in an airtight tin. Not suitable for freezing.

Variations

Add 1 oz (30 g) of sunflower seeds with the oats.

Replace the golden syrup with 4 oz (115 g) of apricot jam.

Cranberry and Orange Squares

Feel festive all year round. Makes 18 small squares

1	large orange	1
6 oz	soft butter	170 g
6 oz	light soft brown sugar	170 g
8 oz	self-raising flour	225 g
1½ tsp	baking powder	7.5 ml
3	large free-range eggs, beaten	3
4 oz	dried cranberries	110 g
1 tbsp	Demerara sugar	15 ml

Preheat your oven to 175ºC (165-170ºC fan). Line a 9x12 inch (22.5x30 cm) roasting tin with non-stick foil or baking paper. *Tip* – wet the tin to help it stick.

Finely grate off all the orange zest into a large bowl. Cut the orange in half, squeeze out the juice and reserve.

Add the butter and light soft brown sugar to the orange zest, and beat together. Tip – you might want to sieve the sugar to break down any lumps.

Sift over the flour and baking powder. Stir in the eggs and 3 tbsp (45 ml) of orange juice. Mix thoroughly but gently until combined. Fold in the dried cranberries.

Spoon the mixture into the tin and smooth the top. Bake for about 30-35 minutes until golden brown, well risen and springy to the touch. Test with a cocktail stick – it should come out clean. Switch off the oven.

Brush the hot cake with a little of the remaining orange juice and sprinkle with the Demerara sugar. Return to the cooling oven for 5 minutes, then take out the cake and allow it cool in the tin.

When cold, cut the cake into 18 squares.

Variation

Replace the cranberries with chopped dried figs.

Fruity Muesli Bars

Only four ingredients. Makes 12 bars

4 oz	chunky marmalade	115 g
4 oz	butter	115 g
1 oz	Demerara sugar	30 g
10 oz	muesli	285 g

Preheat your oven to 200ºC (190ºC fan). Line a 8x10 inch (20x25 cm) roasting tin with non-stick foil or baking paper. *Tip* – wet the tin to help it stick.

Melt the marmalade, butter and Demerara sugar in a pan over a low heat, stir and allow to cool a little. Add the muesli and mix very well.

Empty the mixture into the tin and spread level. *Tip* – push any dried fruit below the surface of the muesli or it will get singed. Bake for about 20 minutes, turning the tin round once, or until golden brown. Mark into 12 bars while still warm and leave to cool in the tin.

Cook's notes

The bars keep well for a week or so in an airtight tin. Not suitable for freezing.

Don't use granola type muesli, it's too crunchy and could become burnt.

Make it a little lighter

Use muesli without added sugar. Bake the mixture in a 9 inch (22.5 cm) square tin and mark into 16 pieces.

Variation

Add 1 oz (30 g) of chopped nuts or shredded coconut with the muesli. Coconut will give the bars a sweeter, crunchier finish.

Almond Biscuits

Even nicer than shortbread. Makes about 24 biscuits

12 oz	plain flour	340 g
2 oz	ground rice	55 g
2 oz	ground almonds	55 g
6oz	salted butter, cubed	170 g
4 oz	golden caster sugar	110 g
1	large free-range egg, beaten	1
	blanched almonds (optional)	

Preheat your oven to 175ºC (160-165ºC fan). Line two baking trays with non-stick foil or baking paper.

Sift the flour into a large bowl and stir in the ground rice and ground almonds. Rub in the butter until the mixture looks like breadcrumbs. Stir through the caster sugar.

Work in the egg, to produce a stiff dough. You can add a few drops of water if necessary, but don't overwork the dough or the biscuits will be tough.

Roll out the dough to a half finger width between two sheets of non-stick baking paper.

Cut out biscuit shapes of your choice and transfer them to the trays. Press a blanched almond into the top of each biscuit if you wish.

Bake for 20-30 minutes until golden brown, turning the trays round halfway through the cooking time.

Lift the biscuits carefully onto a wire rack with a fish slice and allow to cool.

Store in an airtight container.

Cook's notes

The biscuits should keep well for about a week. Can be frozen but may become soft on thawing.

Variations

Replace the ground rice with fine semolina.

Half dip the biscuits in melted chocolate once cool, then leave to set before eating.

Ginger Fairings

Traditional crunchy Cornish biscuits. Makes 12-14 biscuits

2 oz	butter	55 g
2 tbsp	golden syrup	30 ml
4 oz	plain flour	110 g
1 tsp	bicarbonate of soda	5 ml
1 tsp	baking powder	5 ml
1 tsp	ground ginger	5 ml
1 tsp	mixed spice	5 ml
1 tsp	cinnamon	5 ml
2 oz	Demerara sugar	55 g
1 oz	candied lemon peel, chopped	30 g

Preheat your oven to 170ºC (160ºC fan). Line a baking tray with non-stick baking paper.

Melt the butter and golden syrup in a pan over a low heat, stir and allow to cool a little. Add all the remaining ingredients to the pan and mix very well.

Pinch off pieces of the dough about the size of whole walnuts and roll them into balls. Place on the baking tray and flatten out into rounds about half a little finger thickness, allowing room for the biscuits to spread.

Bake for about 15-18 minutes, or until the tops of the biscuits are browned and cracking, as is traditional. Switch off the oven, leaving the biscuits inside with the door ajar for 5-10 minutes more. Remove from the oven and allow to cool completely on the tray.

Cook's notes

Try to find lemon peel in one piece and cut it up yourself. *Tip –* scissors are easiest for this.

The biscuits keep well for a week or so in an airtight tin. Not suitable for freezing.

Variation

Replace the candied lemon peel with 1 tsp (5 ml) freshly grated lemon zest.

6   Best sellers

Cakes to enjoy making and eating again and again.

Iced lemon drizzle cake

Carrot cake

Chocolate fudge cake

Sticky gingerbread

Coffee fudge cake

Iced Lemon Drizzle Cake

My all-time top seller. Makes 1 cake (8-10 slices)

Sponge

2	large lemons (or 3 small ones)	2
6 oz	soft butter	170 g
6 oz	golden caster sugar	170 g
8 oz	self-raising flour	225 g
1½ tsp	baking powder	7.5 ml
3	large free-range eggs, beaten	3
3 tbsp	milk	45 ml

Icing

9 oz	icing sugar, plus a little extra	255 g
2 oz	soft butter	55 g

Preheat your oven to 175ºC (165-170ºC fan). Butter two 8 inch (20 cm) round sandwich tins or use non-stick paper cake tin liners.

Roll the lemons on the worktop to make them more juicy and then finely grate off all the zest into a dish.

For the lemon sponge, put three quarters of the zest into a roomy bowl with the 6 oz (170 g) of soft butter and the caster sugar. Beat together until light and fluffy. Sift over the flour and baking powder. Stir in the eggs and milk. Mix thoroughly but gently until combined.

Divide the mixture equally between the sandwich tins and smooth the tops of the cakes. Bake for about 27-30 minutes until golden brown, well risen and springy to the touch. Test with a cocktail stick – it should come out clean.

While the cakes are baking, squeeze the juice from the lemons into a sieve over a measuring jug. For every 2 tbsp (30 ml) of juice, add 1 tbsp (15 ml) of icing sugar and then stir until all the sugar dissolves.

As soon as the cakes come out of the oven, prick them all over with a cocktail stick and drizzle over 5-6 spoonfuls of the lemon syrup, reserving the remaining syrup. Allow the cakes to cool completely in the tins, or they may break when being turned out.

When the cakes are cold, remove them from the tins. Lay one of them, drizzled top side down, on a plate.

For the filling, cream the 2 oz (55 g) of soft butter with 5 oz (140 g) of icing sugar, the remaining lemon zest and 1-2 spoonfuls of the reserved lemon syrup in a roomy bowl until it forms a soft buttercream. Spread over the cake on the plate. Place the second cake over the buttercream, drizzled top side uppermost.

In a clean bowl, or jug, mix 4 oz (115 g) of icing sugar with enough of the remaining lemon syrup to make a thick, spreadable icing. Pour the icing onto the top of the cake and gently encourage it to the edges with the back of a spoon. Leave the icing to set before cutting the cake.

Cook's notes

The cake keeps well for 3-4 days in an airtight container. Can be frozen if well wrapped, though the icing on top may soften.

Variation

For an orangey cake, replace the 2 lemons with 1 large orange and 1 small lemon. For the syrup, use 1 tsp (5 ml) icing sugar per 1 tbsp (15 ml) mixed orange and lemon juice in the syrup.

Carrot Cake

A very moist cake with a soft vanilla topping. Makes 1 cake (8 wedges)

Cake

8 oz	self-raising flour	225 g
2 tsp	baking powder	10 ml
1 tsp	mixed spice	5 ml
½ tsp	ground cinnamon	2.5 ml
½ tsp	grated nutmeg (optional)	2.5 ml
5 oz	dark soft brown sugar	140 g
1-2 oz	chopped pecan nuts	30-55 g
9 oz	grated carrot	255 g
2	large free-range eggs, beaten	2
5 fluid oz	corn oil	140 ml

Buttercream

2 oz	soft butter	55 g
5 oz	icing sugar	140 g
½ tsp	vanilla extract	2.5 ml
2 tsp	cooled boiled water	10 ml
8	pecan nut halves	8

Preheat your oven to 180ºC (170ºC fan). Butter and flour a deep 8 inch (20 cm) round tin or use a non-stick paper cake tin liner.

Sift the flour, baking powder and spices into a bowl. Stir in the sugar, breaking up any clumps. Add the nuts and grated carrot, and stir until the carrot shreds are well coated with flour. Add the eggs and oil, and mix thoroughly.

Spoon the mixture into the tin and bake for about 50-60 minutes, or until a skewer comes out clean. Allow to cool almost completely in the tin before transferring to a cooling rack.

For the buttercream, beat the butter, icing sugar, vanilla extract and water together until light and creamy. Swirl the buttercream on top of the cake. Decorate with the pecan halves.

Cook's notes

The cake can be frozen without the topping.

Make it a little lighter

Reduce the sugar content by 1 oz (30 g) and omit the topping. Hand reduced-fat crème fraîche separately rather than putting it on the cake.

Variations

Use walnuts instead of pecan nuts.

Swap the vanilla buttercream topping for the soft cheese frosting on page 14. Swirl over the top of the cake and decorate with nuts. In this case, the cake is best eaten within two days, but do keep it in the fridge.

For a nut-free version, replace the chopped nuts in the cake with raisins, and decorate the top of the finished cake with white chocolate buttons.

Chocolate Fudge Cake

Darkly delicious. Makes 1 large cake (10 slices)

Cake

10 oz	self-raising flour	285 g
4 tbsp	cocoa powder	60 ml
1 tsp	bicarbonate of soda	5 ml
3 oz	dark soft brown sugar	85 g
3 oz	Demerara sugar	85 g
5 fluid oz	corn oil	140 ml
10 fluid oz	milk	280 ml
2 tbsp	golden syrup	30 ml

Fudge icing

9 oz	icing sugar	255 g
1 oz	cocoa powder	30 g
4 oz	soft butter	110 g
	warm boiled water	
	white chocolate buttons or stars	

Preheat your oven to 180ºC (170ºC fan). Butter two 9 inch (22.5 cm) round sandwich tins or use non-stick paper cake tin liners.

Sift the flour, cocoa powder and bicarbonate of soda into a large bowl. Stir in the sugars, making sure there are no clumps. Add the oil and milk, and mix gently but thoroughly. Stir in the syrup. The mixture should be a soft dropping consistency, but if not you can add a little more milk. Divide the batter evenly between the tins and smooth the tops.

Bake the cakes for about 25-27 minutes, until well risen and springy to the touch. Test with a cocktail stick – it should come out clean. Cool for at least 10 minutes in the tins before transferring to a cooling rack, or the cakes may crack.

For the fudge icing, put the icing sugar, cocoa powder and butter in a roomy bowl and add a couple of tablespoons of water. *Tip* – use warm not hot water or the icing may become grainy. Beat until the icing is shiny.

Working quickly, before the fudge icing sets, sandwich the cold cakes together with half the icing and swirl the remainder on top. Decorate with white chocolate buttons or stars.

Serve with whipped cream or crème fraîche if you fancy.

Cook's notes

A food processor takes the hard work out of making the fudge icing.

The cake will keep for up to a week in an airtight container.

Make it a little lighter

Reduce the sugar content by 1 oz (30 g), make only half the quantity of fudge icing and use it to sandwich the cakes. Serve with plain fat-free yoghurt.

Sticky Gingerbread

Good at any time of day. Makes 1 cake (12 pieces)

Cake

6 oz	butter	170 g
7 oz	dark soft brown sugar	200 g
2 tbsp	honey or black treacle	30 ml
1–2 tbsp	marmalade, chopped finely	15-30 ml
½ oz	glacé ginger, chopped finely	15 g
9 oz	plain flour	225 g
1 tsp	baking powder	5 ml
2 tsp	bicarbonate of soda	10 ml
3 tsp	ground ginger	15 ml
1 tsp	mixed spice	5 ml
1	large free-range egg, beaten	1
5 fluid oz	milk	140 ml

Icing

1½ oz	icing sugar	40 g
½ oz	glacé ginger, chopped finely	15 g
	citrus juice or boiled water	

Preheat your oven to 160ºC (150-155ºC fan). Line a 10 inch round (25 cm), or 9 inch square (22.5 cm) cake tin with baking paper or non-stick foil. *Tip* – wet the tin to help it stick.

Put the butter, sugar, honey or treacle, marmalade and glacé ginger in a pan over a low heat to melt, and stir thoroughly to blend. Allow to cool, almost to room temperature (this is important).

Sift the flour, baking powder, bicarbonate of soda, ginger and mixed spice into a bowl. Add the melted ingredients gradually to the sifted ones and mix well. Add the egg and milk and mix again.

Pour the batter into the tin and bake for about 45-55 minutes, or until a skewer comes out clean. Allow to cool completely in the tin before turning out.

To decorate the cake, mix the icing sugar with enough freshly squeezed orange or lemon juice, or cooled boiled water, to create a runny icing. Drizzle the icing over the top of the cake in squiggly lines of graffiti and scatter over the chopped glacé ginger Leave to set.

The gingerbread is best left overnight, in an airtight container (not the fridge), before cutting.

Cook's notes

Don't worry if the cake sinks a little in the middle, gingerbread often does, but it will still taste just as good. The flavour will develop with time.

Keeps well for up to two weeks in an airtight tin.

Variation

For a pale coloured gingerbread with a lighter flavour, use golden syrup in place of the honey or black treacle and golden caster sugar instead of dark soft brown sugar.

Coffee Fudge Cake

Go nutty over this coffee cake. Makes 1 cake (8-10 slices)

Sponge

1½ tbsp	instant coffee granules	22.5 ml
1 oz	walnuts or pecan nuts	30 g
10 oz	self-raising flour	285 g
1 tsp	bicarbonate of soda	5 ml
3 oz	light soft brown sugar	85 g
3 oz	Demerara sugar	85 g
5 fluid oz	corn oil	140 ml
8¾ fluid oz	milk	250 ml
2 tbsp	golden syrup	30 ml

Fudge icing

9 oz	icing sugar	255 g
3½ oz	soft butter	100 g
1 tbsp	instant coffee granules	15 ml
	walnut or pecan nut halves	

Preheat your oven to 180ºC (170ºC fan). Butter two 8 inch (20 cm) round sandwich tins or use non-stick paper cake tin liners.

Dissolve the coffee granules in 2 tbsp (30 ml) boiling water and set aside. Finely chop or grind the nuts for the sponge and put into a large bowl. Sift over the flour, bicarbonate of soda and light soft brown sugar. Stir in the Demerara sugar.

Add the oil, milk and coffee liquid, and mix gently but thoroughly. Stir in the syrup. The mixture should be a soft dropping consistency, but if not you can add a little more milk. Divide the batter evenly between the tins and smooth the tops.

Bake the cakes for about 25-27 minutes, until well risen and springy to the touch. Test with a cocktail stick – it should come out clean. Cool for at least 20 minutes in the tins before transferring to a cooling rack, or the cakes may crack.

For the fudge icing, dissolve the coffee granules in 1 tbsp (15 ml) of warm boiled water in the bottom of a roomy bowl. Add the icing sugar and butter, and beat until the icing is soft and fluffy.

Sandwich the cold cakes together with half the icing and swirl the remainder on top. Decorate with the nut halves.

Cook's notes

A food processor takes the hard work out of chopping the nuts and making the fudge icing.

The cake will keep for up to a week in an airtight container.

Make it a little lighter

Reduce the sugar content by 1 oz (30 g), make only half the quantity of fudge icing and use it to sandwich the cakes. Serve with plain fat-free yoghurt.

Variation

For a nut-free version, omit the chopped nuts in the sponge, and decorate the top of the finished cake with dark chocolate coffee beans and milk chocolate drops.

7   Old favourites

Delicious cakes that never go out of fashion.

Victoria sandwich

Marble cake

Everyday fruitcake

Lemon syrup cake

Malted fruit loaf

Victoria Sandwich

Reputedly Queen Victoria's teatime favourite. Makes 1 cake (8 slices)

3	large free-range eggs	3
6 oz	soft butter	170 g
6 oz	golden caster sugar	170 g
6 oz	self-raising flour	170 g
6 tbsp	raspberry or strawberry jam	90 ml
	extra golden caster sugar	

Preheat your oven to 180°C (170°C fan). Butter and flour two 8 inch (20 cm) round sandwich tins or use non-stick paper cake tin liners.

Traditionally, the cake should have exactly equal quantities of egg, butter, sugar and flour. If you want make it this way, weigh your three eggs first and use that number as the weight for the other ingredients.

For a really light sponge, first sift your flour into a dish and leave it in the warm kitchen while you start on the cake.

Cream the soft butter and golden caster sugar in a roomy mixing bowl, beating well with a wooden spoon until the mixture is very pale and fluffy. Stir in one beaten egg at a time. If the mixture seems to be curdling, add a spoonful of the flour. When all the eggs are in, fold in the flour as gently as you can, using a large metal spoon. You are trying to keep as much air in the sponge as possible. If the mixture looks a little dry, gently stir in a few drops of warm boiled water.

Divide the mixture equally between the tins and smooth the tops. Bake for 25-30 minutes until pale golden brown, well risen and springy to the touch. A cocktail stick should come out clean.

After 10 minutes, turn the sponges onto a wire rack to cool.

When the cakes are completely cold, sandwich them together with the jam and dust the top with caster sugar.

Cook's notes

The cake is best eaten within a couple of days, and do keep it in an airtight container. Can be frozen if well wrapped.

Variations

Flavour the sponge with grated lemon or orange zest and sandwich the cakes with lemon or orange curd.

For an extra treat, add a layer of whipped cream to the filling.

Marble Cake

Unashamedly retro. Makes 1 cake (8 wedges)

6 oz	soft butter	170 g
6 oz	golden caster sugar	170 g
6 oz	self-raising flour, sifted	170 g
½ oz	cocoa powder, sifted	15 g
3	large free-range eggs, beaten	3
1 tbsp	boiled water, plus a little extra	15 ml

You will need a well-buttered ring mould or a 7 inch (17.5cm) deep round cake tin lined with non-stick baking paper.

Preheat your oven to 180ºC (170ºC fan).

Cream the butter and sugar together in a bowl until light and fluffy. Beat in one of the eggs, then fold in one-third of the flour. Repeat with the remaining eggs and flour. Gently mix in 1 tbsp (15 ml) of hot water.

Put half of the cake mixture into a separate bowl and fold in the cocoa powder. Add a few drops of hot water if the mixture looks dry, it should have the same consistency as the plain batter.

Spoon the two mixtures alternately into the tin, to achieve a marbled effect. Run a cocktail stick briefly through the two mixtures if you wish.

Bake for about 40-50 minutes, depending on the tin used, until well risen and springy to the touch. A cocktail stick should come out clean.

Cool for at least 20 minutes in the tin and then turn out onto a wire rack to finish cooling.

Cook's notes

Marble cake is best eaten within a couple of days.

Any leftover cake makes a good base for a homemade trifle with raspberries, custard, cream and chocolate curls – sherry optional – but, please, no jelly.

Everyday Fruitcake

Every day should have a piece. Makes 1 large cake (16 slices)

2	Earl Grey teabags	2
12 oz	mixed dried fruit	340 g
4 oz	glacé cherries	110 g
1 tbsp	brandy or sherry (optional)	15 ml
1 lb	self-raising flour	450 g
1 tsp	mixed spice	5 ml
¼ tsp	grated nutmeg (optional)	1.25 ml
8 oz	dark soft brown sugar	225 g
2	free-range eggs	2
1 tbsp	golden syrup or black treacle	15 ml

Start the evening before you want to bake the cake. Put the teabags in a heatproof jug and pour over 13 fluid oz (370 ml) of boiling water. Allow to steep for at least 10 minutes to extract maximum flavour.

Cut the glacé cherries in half and put into a non-metallic airtight container with the mixed dried fruit. Pour over the strong tea and brandy or sherry (if using). Stir well and close the lid.

Next day, preheat your oven to 160ºC (150ºC fan). Butter and flour a 9 inch (22.5 cm) deep round cake tin or use a non-stick paper cake tin liner.

Sift the flour, mixed spice and grated nutmeg (if using) into a large bowl. Stir in the sugar, breaking up any clumps. Add the soaked fruit with any liquid, the eggs and the syrup or treacle. Mix very thoroughly. The mixture should drop slightly reluctantly from the spoon but not look dry. If it needs a bit more moisture, you can add a little milk or cold tea.

Spoon the mixture into the tin, levelling the surface and pushing any fruit below the top so it doesn't catch. This cake can take around 2 hours to bake, as much depends upon the moisture levels of the fruit and the fierceness of your oven. Set the timer for 1 hour and 20 minutes and then test the cake with a skewer. If it is ready the skewer should come out clean, but the cake may need up to a further 40 minutes, so test it at intervals.

When the cake is ready, leave it to cool in the tin.

Cook's notes

The fruit cake is best left overnight before cutting. It will keep well for around two weeks in an airtight tin.

Variations

You can make the cake with 1 lb (450 g) of mixed dried fruit and omit the glacé cherries if you prefer.

A slice of sharp salty cheese is a good counterpoint to the sweet cake. Or you might like to serve it sliced and buttered as a tea bread.

Lemon Syrup Cake

Light, lemony and sticky. Makes 1 cake (12-16 pieces)

2	large lemons (or 3 small ones)	2
6 oz	soft butter	170 g
6 oz	golden caster sugar	170 g
8 oz	self-raising flour	225 g
1½ tsp	baking powder	7.5 ml
¼ tsp	ground mace (optional)	1.25 ml
3	large free-range eggs, beaten	3
3 tbsp	milk	45 ml
	extra golden caster sugar	

Preheat your oven to 175ºC (165-170ºC fan). Line a 9 inch (22.5 cm) square cake tin with non-stick foil or baking paper. *Tip* – wet the tin to help it stick.

Finely grate off all the lemon zest into a roomy bowl. Add the butter and sugar, and beat to combine. Sift over the flour, baking powder and ground mace (if using). Stir in the eggs and milk. Mix thoroughly but gently.

Spoon the mixture into the tin, spreading it right to the corners and smooth the top. Bake for about 30 minutes until golden brown, well risen and springy to the touch. A cocktail stick should come out clean.

While the cake is baking, squeeze the juice from the lemons into a measuring jug, discarding any pips. For every 1 tbsp (15 ml) of juice, add 2 tsp (10 ml) of golden caster sugar. Pour the lemon juice and sugar into a small pan and heat, stirring, until all the sugar dissolves.

As soon as the cake comes out of the oven, prick it all over with a cocktail stick and pour over all the lemon syrup. Allow the cake to cool completely in its tin. When cold, turn out carefully as it may break, and cut into 12 or 16 pieces.

Cook's notes

Mace is the outer wrapping of a nutmeg kernel. It imparts an aromatic citrus flavour that intensifies the lemon in the cake.

The cake keeps well for up to a week in an airtight container. Can be frozen if well wrapped.

Malted Fruit Loaf

Low fat indulgence, and less sugar. Makes 1 loaf (8-10 slices)

6 oz	self-raising flour	170 g
½ tsp	mixed spice	2.5 ml
3 tbsp	malt drink (plain or chocolate)	45 ml
1 oz	dark soft brown sugar	30 g
3 oz	sultanas	85 g
2 tbsp	black treacle	30 ml
5 fluid oz	milk	140 ml

Preheat your oven to 180ºC (170ºC fan). Butter and flour a small loaf tin or use a non-stick paper loaf tin liner.

Sift the flour, mixed spice and malt drink powder into a bowl. Stir in the sugar and sultanas. Mix in the treacle and milk, forming a thick batter.

Spoon the mixture into the tin, smoothing the top and pushing any sultanas under the surface so they don't burn. Bake for 50-60 minutes, or until a skewer comes out clean. Leave in the tin for at least 10 minutes and then turn out onto a cooling rack.

Serve in slices, either on its own or spread with butter, cream cheese or homemade lemon curd – or all three! It's up to your waistline.

Cook's notes

The malt loaf keeps well for a week or so in an airtight tin.

Variations

Try raisins or mixed dried fruit instead of sultanas.

8   Scones and savouries

When you just don't feel like cake.

Afternoon tea scones

Easy cheesy scones

Quick pastry

Mini salmon quiches

Carrot, cheese and mustard flan

Cheese and poppy seed shortbreads

Seeded soda bread

Afternoon Tea Scones

A teatime favourite. Makes about 6 large scones

8 oz	plain flour	225 g
½ tsp	cream of tartar	2.5 ml
½ tsp	bicarbonate of soda	2.5 ml
1½ oz	butter	40 g
1 oz	golden caster sugar	30 g
1 tsp	lemon juice	5 ml
¼ pint	milk	140 ml
	beaten free range egg to glaze	

Preheat your oven to 230ºC (215ºC fan). Line a baking tray with non-stick baking parchment.

Sift the flour, cream of tartar and bicarbonate of soda into a mixing bowl. Using only your fingertips, rub in the butter until the mixture looks like breadcrumbs. Stir in the sugar.

Sour the milk with the lemon juice. Add three quarters of the milk to the dry ingredients. Work into a soft, but not wet, dough with a round bladed knife or your hand, adding more liquid if necessary.

Turn the dough onto a floured surface (*Tip* – use a piece of baking paper on the worktop) handling it just enough so that it comes together in a ball. Pat it out to about thumb width.

Cut out 2 in (5 cm) rounds, reshaping the trimmings to make more, and place on the baking tray. *Tip* – don't twist the cutter as you stamp out the scones, or they may rise lopsidedly.

Brush the tops of the scones with beaten egg. Pop into the oven for 10–15 minutes until well risen and golden brown, turning the tray round halfway through. They are done when they sound hollow if tapped on the underside. Transfer to a cooling rack.

Good spread with butter and marmalade or topped with jam and clotted cream (the cream goes on the top in Cornwall!).

Cook's notes

Best eaten on the day of making, ideally when still warm.

Variations

Plump up 1 oz (30 g) of sultanas in a little Earl Grey tea, drain and add to the scone mix with the liquid.

Stir in 1 oz (30 g) of chopped glacé cherries or candied peel with the liquid.

Try half and half wholemeal flour with white flour, and use light soft brown sugar instead of golden caster sugar.

Easy Cheesy Scones

Irresistible served warm. Makes 8-12, depending on size

8 oz	plain flour	225 g
½ tsp	salt (optional)	2.5 ml
1 tsp	English mustard powder	5 ml
3 tsp	baking powder	15 ml
1 oz	butter	30 g
6 oz	mature Cheddar, grated	170 g
1	large free-range egg, beaten	1
1 tsp	vinegar or lemon juice	5 ml
¼ pint	milk or water	140 ml

Preheat your oven to 220ºC (205ºC fan). Line a baking tray with non-stick baking parchment.

Sift the flour, salt (if using), mustard and baking powder into a mixing bowl. Using only your fingertips, rub in the butter until the mixture looks like breadcrumbs. Mix in about 5 oz (140 g) of the grated cheese.

Stir in the egg, the vinegar or lemon juice and half the milk or water. Work into a soft dough with a round bladed knife or your hand, adding more liquid if necessary. The dough should be soft but not sticky.

Turn the dough onto a floured surface (*Tip* – use a piece of baking paper on the worktop) and pat it out to about finger width. Cut out rounds of the size you like and place on the baking tray. Bring together the scraps to cut out more scones. *Tip* – don't twist the cutter as you stamp out the scones, or they may rise lopsidedly.

Brush the scones with milk or water and sprinkle with the remaining cheese. Bake for 10–15 minutes until well risen and golden brown, turning the tray round halfway through. They are done when they sound hollow if tapped on the underside. Transfer to a cooling rack.

Eat as they are, with butter or filled with soft cheese and chopped fresh coriander.

Cook's notes

Best eaten fresh, while still warm.

Make it a little lighter

Use a well-flavoured low-fat hard cheese instead of Cheddar.

Variations

Try wholemeal flour, or half and half with white flour, and Stilton instead of Cheddar.

Quick Pastry

A food processor is your friend here.

8 oz	plain flour	225 g
4 oz	salted butter, cubed	115 g
	boiled water	

This is my method of making quick shortcrust pastry. It does away with chilling and – so far – has produced golden pastry that won't shrink in the oven.

It's important that both the butter and the water are at room temperature. I find that if the butter is hard, it takes much more work to rub it into the flour. That in turn overworks the flour, making the gluten in it elastic. Elasticity is great in bread dough but not if you want crumbly melt-in-your-mouth pastry. Water is also no friend to pastry – the more you add, the tougher it gets. And because cold ingredients don't amalgamate as well as warm ones, you need to add more water, if it's cold, to get the paste to stick together.

A food processor cuts down the mixing time, which further helps to reduce the danger of over working the flour's gluten. But you can make the pastry by hand too, just handle it as little as you possibly can.

Quickly blitz the flour and butter to crumbs, using the pulse function on the processor.

Add a couple of tablespoons of water and pulse again. You may need more water, so add it a little at a time. How much you need depends upon how dry your flour is and how moist your butter – different brands do vary.

The pastry is ready when most of the crumbs have clumped together. If you squeeze some of the paste it should feel soft but not grainy.

Tip the pastry out onto a large sheet of non-stick paper and shape into a disc. Top with a second sheet of non-stick paper, and you're ready to roll. You can use the pastry straightaway, or leave it to rest at room temperature for 10 minutes. If you're not ready to use it by then, pop it in the fridge – wrapped in non-PVC cling film – but do allow the pastry to return to room temperature before you roll.

Cook's notes

Raw pastry can be frozen if well wrapped. Thaw and use at room temperature.

Mini Salmon Quiches

Luxury on a budget, tastes good hot or cold. Makes 5-8 mini quiches

Pastry

6 oz	plain flour	170 g
3 oz	salted butter, cubed	85 g
	boiled water	

Filling

3¾ oz	tin of red salmon	105 g
3½ oz	light soft cheese	100 g
3	large free-range eggs	3
9½ fluid oz	milk	270 ml
1 tbsp	chopped fresh herbs	15 ml

You will need 6 individual tins of 3.5 inch (8.5 cm) in diameter, or two Yorkshire pudding trays. Make the pastry according to the method on page 50. Roll it out thinly and line the tins with circles of pastry slightly larger than the hollows. *Tip* – cut round a saucer. Set aside while you make the filling.

Preheat your oven to 200ºC (190ºC fan).

Drain the salmon, reserving the can juices. Remove and discard all skin and bones. Flake the fish into a bowl, add the soft cheese and about 1 tbsp (15 ml) of the salmon juices, mix well. Beat the eggs and milk together. Add to the salmon mixture with the herbs and stir well.

If using individual tins, put them on a baking tray. Pour the filling into the pastry cases. *Tip* – spoon in the last bit when the tins are in the oven to prevent spills. Bake for about 20-22 minutes until puffed up, browned and just set in the middle.

Cook's notes

Choose fish from a sustainable source, such as Alaskan salmon.

Variations

Try half and half wholemeal and white flour in the pastry.

Use light soft cheese with added black pepper, chives or chilli to ring the changes.

Carrot, Cheese and Mustard Flan

Great for a picnic. Makes 1 large flan

Pastry

2 oz	wholemeal flour	55 g
5 oz	plain flour	145 g
3½ oz	salted butter, cubed	100 g
	boiled water	

Filling

3	medium carrots	3
3	large free-range eggs	3
6 fluid oz	milk	180 ml
1-2 tsp	Tewkesbury mustard	5-10 ml
3 oz	mature Cheddar cheese, grated	85 g
	freshly ground black pepper	

You will need a 9 inch (22.5 cm) round deep flan dish or sandwich tin. Make the pastry according to the method on page 50. Roll it out thinly enough to line the tin with pastry and let it rest (without trimming the edges) while you make the filling.

Put a baking tray in your oven and preheat it to 215ºC (200ºC fan).

Peel and grate the carrots finely, or whizz them in a food processor until chopped very small. Add all the remaining filling ingredients, season and mix until well blended.

Trim the edges of the pastry. Remove the baking tray from the oven and place the flan dish on it. Pour the filling carefully into the pastry case. *Tip* – spoon in the last bit when the tin is in the oven to prevent spills. Bake for about 30 minutes until puffed up, browned and just set in the middle.

Serve hot, topped with a sprinkle of toasted pine kernels and/or hot crispy bacon.

Cook's notes

Tewkesbury mustard is a delicious mild mustard with added horseradish. If you can't find it in the shops, try Dijon or grainy mustard instead.

Will keep for a couple of days in the fridge, but only reheat the flan once.

Make it a little lighter

Use a well-flavoured low-fat hard cheese instead of Cheddar.

Variations

Try blue or goat's cheese instead of Cheddar.

Cheese and Poppy Seed Shortbreads

Impossible to eat just one. Makes about 20 savoury biscuits

3 oz	plain flour	85 g
½ tsp	paprika	2.5 ml
¼ tsp	freshly ground black pepper	1.25 ml
2 oz	salted butter, cubed	55 g
1 oz	ground almonds	30 g
1½ oz	cheese, grated finely	40 g
2 tbsp	poppy seeds	30 ml
1	free-range egg, separated	1
	extra cheese to sprinkle, optional	

Preheat your oven to 175ºC (160-165ºC fan). Line two baking trays with non-stick baking parchment.

Sift the flour, paprika and black pepper into a bowl. Rub in the butter to the crumbly breadcrumb stage. Stir in the ground almonds, grated cheese and poppy seeds.

Mix in the egg yolk to form a soft dough. Roll it out between two sheets of non-stick paper or cling film to about half a finger width. Cut out 2 inch (5 cm) rounds and lay them on the baking trays.

Lightly beat the egg white and brush over the biscuits. Sprinkle with a little extra crated cheese if you wish.

Bake for 10-15 minutes until golden brown. Remove to a wire rack after 10 minutes on the trays.

Cook's notes

You can use smoked or sweet paprika here, whichever you like best.

Use an extra mature Cheddar, Pecorino or Parmesan cheese to give the shortbreads a good flavour.

Variation

Swap the ground almonds for fine semolina if you prefer a nut-free version.

Alternatively, replace the flour and ground almonds with 4 oz (115 g) of spelt flour. You may need to add a small knob of extra butter to get the mixture to bind.

Seeded Soda Bread

Good with soup or cheese. Makes 1 loaf (8 pieces)

4½ oz	wholemeal flour	130 g
7 oz	plain flour	200 g
1½ tsp	bicarbonate of soda	7.5 ml
1½ tsp	cream of tartar	7.5 ml
	pinch of sea salt	
	pinch of Cayenne pepper	
1½ oz	pumpkin seeds	40 g
1½ oz	sunflower seeds	40 g
1 tbsp	poppy seeds	15 ml
1 tbsp	sesame or flax seeds	15 ml
1½ oz	Parmesan cheese, grated	40 g
8 fluid oz	buttermilk	225 ml
1 tbsp	olive oil	15 ml

Preheat your oven to 195ºC (185ºC fan). Line a baking tray with non-stick baking parchment.

Sift the flours, bicarbonate of soda, cream of tartar, salt and cayenne pepper into a large bowl. Mix in all the seeds and the grated Parmesan. Add the buttermilk and olive oil.

Work into a soft dough with a round-bladed knife, adding a little milk if it seems dry. Knead the dough briefly so it forms a ball, and transfer to the baking tray. Wet your hands and pat the dough into a circle about as thick as your thumb. Mark the surface into eight wedges with a knife.

Bake for 40-45 minutes until golden brown. Transfer to a cooling rack.

Best served slightly warm, or split and toasted the next day.

Variations

Try making the bread with granary flour and experiment with different seeds – such as linseeds or sesame seeds in place of the poppy seeds.

9   Proper puddings

A fitting end to a meal, or an afternoon treat.

Almondy tart

Marmalade bread and butter pudding

Fruit crumble

Individual raspberry puddings

Baked stone fruit

Libby's deep-filled treacle tart

Apple and ginger dessert cakes

Almondy Tart

My version of a Bakewell pudding. Makes 1 tart (8 slices)

Pastry

6 oz	plain flour	170 g
2¾ oz	butter, cubed	80 g
2 tsp	icing sugar	10 ml
	boiled water	

Filling

3¾ oz	butter	105 g
3¾ oz	golden caster sugar	105 g
3½ oz	ground almonds	100 g
1 oz	ground rice	30 g
2	free-range eggs, beaten	2
4 tbsp	raspberry jam	60 ml
	flaked almonds	

Icing (optional)

1½ oz	icing sugar	40 g
	citrus juice or boiled water	

You will need an 8 inch (20 cm) round flan dish or sandwich tin. Make the pastry according to the method on page 50, adding the icing sugar to the flour. Roll it out thinly enough to line the tin with pastry and let it rest (without trimming the edges) while you make the filling.

Put a baking tray in your oven and preheat it to 200ºC (190ºC fan).

Melt the butter for the filling in a pan. Add the sugar, ground almonds and ground rice and stir well. Trim the edges of the pastry and prick the base with a fork (this stops it lifting up during baking). Spread the raspberry jam over the pricked base.

Gradually beat the eggs into the filling mixture. Pour the filling into the pastry case and sprinkle the top with flaked almonds. Bake for about 35 minutes until the filling is golden brown all over. You may need to turn the tin round halfway through to ensure an even colour.

Serve warm or cold, but cool in the tin.

If you want to ice the tart, mix the icing sugar with enough freshly squeezed orange or lemon juice, or cooled boiled water, to create a runny icing. Drizzle squiggles of icing over the top of the tart and leave to set.

Eat the tart just as it is, or pair it with clotted cream, crème fraîche, ice cream or custard.

Cook's notes

Can be frozen without the icing.

Variation

Make a lemony tart by spreading the pastry with lemon curd instead of jam and adding the grated zest of a lemon to the filling. Omit the flaked almonds on top of the tart and decorate it with icing made with lemon juice and 2 oz (55 g) icing sugar.

Marmalade Bread and Butter Pudding

A bit of wobbliness is a good thing here. Makes 4-6 helpings

3	small soft bread rolls	3
1-2 oz	soft butter	30-55 g
4 tbsp	thin-cut marmalade	60 ml
1 pint	creamy milk	570 ml
½ tsp	vanilla extract	2.5 ml
	pinch of sea salt	
3	large free-range eggs	3
1 oz	light soft brown sugar	30 g

Butter an ovenproof dish of 2 pint (1.2 litres) capacity. Slice the rolls thinly, spread with the butter and marmalade and arrange in overlapping rows in the dish.

Whisk the eggs and sugar together in a large heatproof jug. Heat the milk, vanilla extract and salt to boiling point in a pan. Pour over the egg and sugar mixture, whisking again.

Strain the custard through a sieve onto the bread slices. Cover the dish and leave it to stand at room temperature for about 1 hour.

Preheat your oven to 200ºC (190ºC fan). Boil a full kettle of water.

Uncover the pudding and place the dish in a large roasting tin. Put the whole lot in the oven and pour boiling water into the roasting tin until it comes halfway up the sides of the dish.

Bake for 35-45 minutes, or until the top is golden brown but the pudding still has a slight wobble. *Tip* – use a knife to check there is no uncooked custard at the bottom.

Serve hot, warm or cold. Chilled cream is a good accompaniment.

Cook's notes

You can use white or wholemeal rolls but not grainy ones. Alternatively use 4-6 thin slices of bread without crusts.

When made with brown bread this is also called Osborne pudding. The name may be a reference to Osborne House, Queen Victoria's residence on the Isle of Wight, where it was served to her majesty.

Make it a little lighter

Halve the quantities of butter, marmalade and sugar, and add grated orange zest and a pinch of cinnamon to the custard for sweetness. Serve without cream.

Variation

Swap the bread rolls for hot cross buns and omit the sugar.

Fruit Crumble

Warming and comforting on a cold day. Makes 6 helpings

1 lb 4 oz	cooking apples	570 g
1-2 tbsp	golden caster sugar	15-30 ml
8 oz	blackberries or blueberries	225 g
3 oz	butter	85 g
5 oz	rolled or porridge oats	140 g
3 oz	flour	85 g
3 oz	Demerara sugar	85 g

Preheat your oven to 180ºC (170ºC fan).

Peel, core and slice the apples into a large ovenproof dish. Sprinkle with the caster sugar and a few drops of water. Cover the dish with foil and bake for 15 minutes.

Meanwhile melt the butter in a roomy pan and stir in the oats. Sift over the flour and mix well, then stir in the sugar.

Take the apples out of the oven and stir through the berries. Scatter the crumble topping evenly over the fruit. Bake uncovered for 25-30 minutes, or until crisp and golden on top. Set aside for 10 minutes if eating hot, longer if eating warm.

Serve with chilled cream or hot custard.

Cook's notes

Not suitable for freezing.

Make it a little lighter

Use only half the quantity of crumble topping and serve with thick plain yoghurt instead of cream or custard.

Variation

Store cupboard crumble – replace the fresh fruit and caster sugar with three tins of fruit that has been canned in natural juice. Well-drained apricot halves, peach halves or pineapple cubes work well. Taste the fruit first and if it is sweet, reduce the Demerara sugar in the topping to 2 oz (55 g). There is no need to pre-bake the fruit.

Individual Raspberry Puddings

A taste of summer all year round. Makes 4 puddings

8 oz	fresh or frozen raspberries	225 g
3 oz	self-raising flour	85 g
½ tsp	baking powder	2.5 ml
2 oz	golden caster sugar	55 g
2 oz	soft butter	55 g
1	large free-range egg	1
	few drops rose water	
	few drops pink food colour (optional)	

You will need four 4 inch (10 cm) diameter ovenproof ramekins on a baking tray.

Preheat your oven to 180ºC (170ºC fan).

Divide the raspberries between the ramekins. Sift the flour and baking powder into a bowl, then add the sugar, butter and egg. Beat well until evenly blended. Fold in the rosewater and pink colouring (if using).

Spoon the sponge mixture over the raspberries, smoothing the tops and concealing the fruit. Bake in the oven for 20-30 minutes until the sponge feels firm and springs back when pressed. *Tip* – it's better to err on the well-baked side here, as the fruit adds moisture to the mix.

Serve warm rather than hot, liberally dredged with icing sugar, perhaps partnered by clotted cream or ice cream.

Cook's notes

If you use frozen raspberries, make sure they have thawed completely.

Not suitable for freezing.

Variation

Try blackberries instead of raspberries. Or, if you can find them, mulberries are sublime.

Baked Stone Fruit

Simple, delicious and full of flavour. Makes 2 helpings, easily doubled

1	large nectarine	1
2	large plums	2
1-2	green cardamom pods	1-2
	pinch ground cinnamon	
	pinch ground cloves	
	pinch grated nutmeg	
5 tbsp	crème fraîche	75 ml
2	ginger biscuits	2

Preheat your oven to 180ºC (170ºC fan).

Halve and stone the fruit and place cut side up in a single layer in an ovenproof dish. If the nectarine is much larger than the plums cut it into quarters instead of halves.

Break open the cardamom pods, retaining the seeds and discarding the green husks. Stir the cardamom seeds and other spices into the crème fraîche. Dollop the mixture over the cut sides of the fruit.

Crush the ginger biscuits to crumbs. *Tip* – put the biscuits in a bag and bash with a rolling pin or meat mallet. Sprinkle the crumbs onto the crème fraîche.

Bake for 8-16 minutes, depending on the ripeness of the fruit. You want the fruit to be soft but not collapsing.

Serve hot or warm.

Cook's notes

Not suitable for freezing.

Make your own ginger biscuits using the recipe for ginger fairings on page 23.

If you're not keen on any of the spices just leave them out. Use a pinch of ground cardamom in place of the pods if you prefer.

Make it a little lighter

Use reduced-fat crème fraîche.

Libby's Deep-Filled Treacle Tart

My Mum's brilliant recipe, strictly for non-dieters. Makes 1 tart

8 oz	shortcrust pastry	225 g
2	large lemons	2
12 oz	golden syrup	340 g
7-8 oz	fresh breadcrumbs	200-225 g

Preheat your oven to 180ºC (170ºC fan).

Roll out the pastry and use it to line a greased loose-base tin, 7 inch (17.5 cm) diameter with sides at least 2 inch (5 cm) deep. Trim the edges of the pastry level with the top of the tin.

Grate the zest from the lemons into a pan and squeeze in their juice, discarding any pips. Add the golden syrup and heat until liquid. Stir in 7 oz (200 g) of the breadcrumbs. If the mixture looks too runny add a few more crumbs. You are aiming for a soft dropping consistency.

Pour the mixture into the pastry case and spread it level. If you wish, use the pastry trimmings to decorate the tart.

Bake for 25-35 minutes, until the pastry is golden brown and the filling firm to the touch.

Allow the tart to cool from hot to warm in the tin before unmoulding.

Cut into 6-8 wedges and serve warm with chilled cream on the side.

Cook's notes

Use white or wholemeal brown bread to make the crumbs, not granary or seeded bread. Ideally, don't use the crusts either.

Make it a little lighter

Make the tart in a shallow 9 inch (22.5 cm) round flan tin, in which case you should get 10-12 small slices. Serve with plain yoghurt instead of cream.

Apple and Ginger Dessert Cakes

Hurrah, dessert AND cake. Makes 4 generous helpings

5¼ oz	plain flour	150 g
2 tsp	baking powder	10 ml
½ tsp	mixed spice	2.5 ml
	pinch grated nutmeg	
2¼ oz	light soft brown sugar	60 g
2	large crisp eating apples	2
2 oz	butter	55 g
1	large free-range egg, beaten	1
3 fluid oz	milk	85 ml
1 oz	glacé ginger, chopped	30 g

Preheat your oven to 190ºC (180ºC fan). Butter a non-stick four-cup Yorkshire pudding tin.

Sift the flour, baking powder, mixed spice, nutmeg and sugar into a large bowl. Melt the butter in a small pan over a low heat and set aside to cool a little. Peel, quarter and core the apples, and slice thinly.

Stir the butter, egg and milk into the sifted ingredients, mixing gently but thoroughly. Fold in the apple slices and glacé ginger, and spoon the mixture equally into the four wells of the tin.

Bake for about 25-30 minutes, or until golden and springy to the touch. Leave in the tin for at least 10 minutes before transferring to a cooling rack.

Serve hot with custard and a sprinkle of nutmeg as a pudding. Or you can eat the cakes just warm or at room temperature with thick cream.

Cook's notes

Best eaten, or frozen, on the day of making.

Make it a little lighter

Divide the mixture between 6-8 buttered wells of a muffin tray, and reduce the cooking time by a few minutes. Serve with skinny custard.

Variation

Replace the apples with four fresh apricots, not too ripe, and leave the skins on.

10   Gluten-free bakes

No wheat, no problem.

Chocolate nut brownies

Almond cake

Melting moments

Coconut and chocolate bars

Apple muffins

Baked falafel

Savoury muffins

Chocolate Nut Brownies

What's not to like. Makes 16 square brownies

3½ oz	bar dark chocolate (50% cocoa)	100 g
3½ oz	bar milk chocolate with hazelnuts	100 g
3 oz	butter	85 g
3¼ oz	self-raising gluten-free flour	90 g
1 oz	cocoa powder	30 g
3 oz	Demerara sugar	85 g
3 oz	dark soft brown sugar	85 g
3	free-range eggs	3
16	white chocolate buttons	16

Preheat your oven to 180ºC (170ºC fan). Line a 9 inch (22.5 cm) square tin with non-stick foil or baking paper. *Tip* – wet the tin to help it stick.

Break the chocolate bars into squares. Melt the chocolates and butter in a pan over a low heat, stir and allow to cool a little.

Sift the gluten-free flour and cocoa powder into a bowl. Stir in the sugars, making sure there are no clumps. Add the eggs and mix well. Tip the melted chocolate and butter into the bowl and mix thoroughly. Pour the batter into the tin and spread right into the corners.

Bake the brownies for about 18-23 minutes, until the top is firm to the touch but gives a little underneath. Test with a cocktail stick – it should come out with a few damp crumbs attached.

Place the white chocolate buttons on top of the brownie mixture in four rows of four – the heat will melt them slightly so they stick.

Allow the brownies to cool completely in the tin. Lift out the whole lot in the foil or paper and cut into 16 squares.

Variation

Add 1 oz (30 g) of sultanas or raisins to the mix.

Almond Cake

Almond heaven. Makes 1 cake (8-10 slices)

Cake

5 oz	golden caster sugar	140 g
4 oz	soft butter	115 g
3	free-range eggs	3
3½ oz	ground almonds	100 g
1½ oz	rice flour or gluten-free flour	40 g

Icing

4 oz	icing sugar	115 g
1	small lemon	1

Preheat your oven to 175ºC (165ºC fan). Line a 7 inch (17.5 cm) deep round cake tin with non-stick baking parchment.

Beat the caster sugar and butter together with a wooden spoon until pale and fluffy. Gently stir in one beaten egg and one-third of the ground almonds. When they have been incorporated, repeat twice for the other eggs and almonds. Finally, fold in the flour with a metal spoon.

Spoon the cake mixture into the tin and smooth the surface. Bake for 40-45 minutes. Test with a wooden skewer – it should come out completely clean. If not, give the cake a few extra minutes in the oven.

Cool for 10 minutes in the tin and then transfer to a wire cooling rack.

For the icing, grate the lemon's zest into a bowl. Add the icing sugar and enough of the lemon's juice to produce a thick paste. Spread the icing over the top of the cold cake.

Serve in thin slices as it is a rich cake.

Make it a little lighter

Omit the icing and serve the cake with plain fat-free yoghurt.

Variation

Replace the lemon in the icing with half an orange.

Melting Moments

Dreamily jammy. Makes about 8, depending on size

2 oz	soft butter	55 g
2 oz	golden caster sugar	55 g
1	large free-range egg	1
1 oz	gluten-free custard powder	30 g
4 oz	gluten-free self-raising flour	110 g
	raspberry jam	

Preheat your oven to 190ºC (180ºC fan). Line a baking tray with non-stick foil or baking paper.

Cream the butter and sugar together until light and fluffy. Beat in the egg. Sift over the gluten-free custard powder and gluten-free self-raising flour, and fold in with a metal spoon.

Scrape the paste into a disposable piping bag fitted with a large star nozzle, and pipe round swirls onto the baking tray. Alternatively, spoon blobs of the paste onto the tray and make a dent in the centre of each one.

Drop ½ tsp (2.5 ml) of raspberry jam into the centre of each melting moment.

Bake near the top of the oven for 15-20 minutes or until pale golden. Cool on a rack.

Cook's notes

Try making the melting moments with different jams. Strong flavours such as blackcurrant, blueberry or marmalade all work well.

Make it a little lighter

Omit the jam and reduce the sugar by one-quarter.

Variation

Add 1 tsp (5 ml) of grated lemon zest to the paste and bake without jam. As soon as the melting moments come out of the oven, top each one with a small blob of lemon curd and allow to cool.

Coconut and Chocolate Bars

Moreishly rich – and not for the waistline-conscious. Makes 12 bars

2 oz	soft butter	55 g
3 oz	light soft brown sugar	85 g
1	free-range egg	1
4 oz	unsweetened desiccated coconut	110 g
1 oz	glacé cherries, chopped	30 g
2 oz	mixed dried fruit	55 g
3½ oz	bar dark chocolate	100 g

Preheat your oven to 180ºC (170ºC fan). Butter an 8 inch (20 cm) square tin and line it with non-stick baking paper.

Cream the butter and sugar together until they form a soft paste. Beat in the egg and work in the desiccated coconut, glacé cherries and dried fruit. Spread the mixture in the tin, pushing it right into the corners. It will be quite a thin layer.

Bake for 15-25 minutes, taking it out of the oven when it is golden brown all over. Coconut cooks quickly so keep checking. Mark into bars and leave to cool in the tin, set over a wire rack.

Break the dark chocolate bar into squares. Put them into a basin over a pan of hot water and wait for the chocolate to melt.

When the coconut mixture is cold, lift out the whole lot in its foil and separate the bars. Using a pastry brush, coat one side of each bar generously with the chocolate and allow it to set before eating.

Cook's notes

These tend to disappear like lightning, but any that are left keep well in an airtight tin. Not suitable for freezing.

Variation

For a different texture, replace half of the desiccated coconut with gluten-free rolled or porridge oats.

Apple Muffins

A good grab-and-go break time snack. Makes 8 muffins

3	large cooking apples	3
2 tbsp	lemon curd	30 ml
3½ oz	self-raising gluten-free flour	100 g
½ tsp	gluten-free baking powder	2.5 ml
½ tsp	mixed spice	2.5 ml
3 oz	Demerara sugar	85 g
2 fluid oz	corn oil	55 ml
1	large free-range egg, beaten	1

Preheat your oven to 180ºC (170ºC fan). Put 8 paper cases into a 12-cup muffin tray.

Peel, core and dice the apples into a mixing bowl. Stir in the lemon curd to coat the apple cubes.

Sift the flour, baking powder and mixed spice over the apples. Add most of the sugar and mix together. Pour in the oil and egg, and stir until there are no clumps of flour.

Divide the mixture between the paper cases and sprinkle over the remaining sugar. Bake for 25-30 minutes, until deep golden and firm. A cocktail stick should come out sticky but clean.

Cool on a wire rack. Best served just warm or at room temperature.

Cook's notes

Not suitable for freezing. Best eaten within two days.

Variation

Replace the three cooking apples with four sharp eating apples.

Baked Falafel

A savoury nibble that can be as hot as you like. Makes 16-24, depending on size

2 tbsp	olive oil	30 ml
2	banana shallots	2
1	carrot (optional)	1
1 tsp	ground coriander	5 ml
1 tsp	ground cumin	5 ml
½-1 tsp	chilli flakes	2.5-5 ml
2	400 g tins of chick peas in water	2
1	lemon	1
1 tsp	dried mixed herbs	5 ml
1 tbsp	tahini	15 ml

Preheat your oven to 200ºC (185ºC fan). Line a baking tray with non-stick baking paper.

Peel and chop the shallots and soften in 1 tbsp (15 ml) of the oil. If using the carrot, peel and grate it and add to the shallots. Stir in the spices and fry until they become aromatic.

Drain and rinse the chick peas and tip them into a large dish. Grate over the lemon's zest. Stir in the shallot mixture. Add the dried herbs, tahini and 1 tbsp (15 ml) of the lemon's juice. Crush everything together with a sturdy fork or a potato masher, or whizz briefly in a food processor. Taste the falafel mix and add more lemon juice if you wish, plus plenty of ground black pepper and a little salt.

Shape the paste into small balls and place on the baking tray. Brush over the remaining olive oil. Bake for 20-25 minutes, turning once, until firm on the outside. Serve hot or cold.

Cook's notes

Not suitable for freezing.

Bind the falafel paste with a little beaten free-range egg or mayonnaise if you find it too crumbly.

Variation

Replace one of the tins of chick peas with 10 oz (285 g) cooked and shelled broad beans, and add some chopped fresh mint to the mixture.

Savoury Muffins

Serve these instead of gluten-free bread. Makes 8 muffins

5¼ oz	gluten-free self-raising flour	150 g
3½ oz	fine cornmeal (polenta)	100 g
2¼ oz	grated cheese	65 g
1 tsp	dried mixed herbs	5 ml
1¾ oz	pitted black olives	50 g
1	baby sweet pepper	1
1	free-range egg, beaten	1
10½ fluid oz	milk	300 ml
2 tbsp	olive oil	30 ml
	extra oil and cornmeal	

Preheat your oven to 180ºC (170ºC fan). Grease 8 wells of a 12-hole muffin tray with oil and coat with cornmeal (polenta), or use a silicon muffin tray.

Mix the flour, cornmeal, grated cheese and herbs in a bowl. Drain and chop the olives, deseed and finely chop the pepper, and add both to the bowl.

Stir in the egg, milk and olive oil. When well mixed, spoon the batter into the prepared muffin wells.

Bake for 20-25 minutes, or until a cocktail stick comes out clean. Cool in the tin for 20 minutes and then unmould carefully with a round-bladed knife.

Best served slightly warm. Lashings of butter optional.

Cook's notes

A mature hard cheese such as Cheddar or Parmesan works well.

If you can't find baby sweet peppers, use one quarter of an ordinary pepper. Orange or red peppers taste best here.

Eat as they are on the day of making, serve split and toasted the next day. Not suitable for freezing.

Variation

Swap the olives for cooked chopped ham if you prefer.

11   Something extra special

Show off your skills with these baked treats – they are much easier to make than you might think!

Apple and elderberry upside-down shortcake

Chocolate roulade

Christmas brandy butter tartlets

Éclairs

Lemon tart

Rich Christmas cake

Christmas cake decorations

Apple and Elderberry Upside-Down Shortcake

An autumnal excuse to go scrumping for apples and scouring the hedgerows for elderberries. Makes 1 cake (6 wedges)

14	large heads of ripe elderberries	14
3 tbsp	runny honey or golden syrup	45 ml
3	large Bramley cooking apples	3
3½ oz	self-raising flour	100 g
½ tsp	baking powder	2.5 ml
½ tsp	mixed spice	2.5 ml
	pinch ground cloves	
3 oz	golden caster sugar	85 g
2 oz	very soft butter	55 g
1	large free-range egg, beaten	1
1 tbsp	milk	15 ml

Rinse the elderberries and remove from the stalks, discarding any that are still green or pink. Put the elderberries in a small non-stick pan with a tiny splash of water and bring to the boil. Simmer for 5 minutes and then rub through a fine sieve.

Wipe out the pan and return the puréed elderberries to it with the honey or golden syrup. Boil uncovered until the elderberries are reduced to a thick liquid.

Preheat your oven to 175°C (165°C fan). Butter a heavy non-stick 8 inch (20 cm) round sandwich tin – not a loose-base one – and put a circle of baking parchment in the bottom. Butter that too.

Peel, core and thinly slice the apples. Put a little of the elderberry syrup into the bottom of the cake tin and arrange a neat layer of apple slices in the tin. Pour over a little more syrup. Continue until all the apples and elderberries are in the tin.

Sift the flour, baking powder, mixed spice and ground cloves into a bowl. Add the sugar, butter, egg and milk, and mix thoroughly. Dot blobs of the mixture over the apples and smooth over carefully.

Bake for 45-50 minutes, until golden and firm to the touch. Cool in the tin before turning out onto a serving plate when just warm or at room temperature.

Serve in wedges with chilled clotted or pouring cream. Greek yoghurt with lemon also makes a good accompaniment.

Cook's notes

If elderberries are not in season you can use a few tbsp of bramble or blackcurrant jam instead. Mix it with a little boiling water and pass through a sieve.

Have a jar of runny honey to hand in case the apple topping is not sweet enough for everyone's taste, then diners can help themselves to a drizzle at the table.

Keeps well for two days in the fridge if tightly covered. Not suitable for freezing.

Variation

Replace the Bramley apples with four firm Conference pears.

Chocolate Roulade

My husband's go-to top favourite, ever. Makes 1 roulade (10 slices)

Sponge

3 oz	dark soft brown sugar	85 g
3	large free-range eggs	3
3 oz	plain flour	85 g
1 oz	cocoa powder, plus a little extra	30 g

Filling

10 fluid oz	double cream	285 ml
2 tbsp	brandy	30 ml

Covering

3½ oz	dark chocolate (70% cocoa)	100 g
1 tbsp	double cream	15 ml
½ oz	unsalted butter	15 g
2 tbsp	boiling water	30 ml

Preheat your oven to 200ºC (190ºC fan). You will need a baking tray with a lip all the way round, lined with non-stick baking parchment.

For a really light sponge, first sift the flour and cocoa powder into a dish and leave it in the warm kitchen while you start on the roulade.

Whip the brown sugar and eggs together in a large bowl until pale, thick and mousse-like. An electric mixer will take the hard work out of all the whisking required here.

Re-sift the flour and cocoa powder over the eggs and sugar, and fold in with a large metal spoon. Make sure there are no pockets of flour and that the batter is a uniform colour.

Pour onto the baking tray and spread out into a rectangle that covers almost all of the tray. Bake for 10-12 minutes or until the sponge springs back when pressed lightly with a fingertip.

While the chocolate sponge is in the oven, dip two clean tea cloths in water and wring out. Spread one tea cloth out on the work surface. Top it with a sheet of baking paper larger than the baking tray and sift over a light dusting of cocoa powder.

When the sponge is cooked, carefully turn it out onto the cocoa-dusted paper. Do not remove the paper it was baked on. Immediately recover the sponge with the baking tray, and then drape over the second damp tea cloth. Leave undisturbed until the sponge is completely cold, which should prevent it cracking when rolled up.

Meanwhile begin making the ganache. Put all the ingredients for the covering in a pan and melt together over a low heat. Stir and set aside.

For the roulade filling, whip the cream and brandy to floppy peaks. *Tip* – be careful not to whip too much as the cream will thicken as you spread it on the sponge.

Uncover the sponge and peel off the paper it was baked on, which is now on top. Score a line across one end of the sponge to help roll it up. Spread over the whipped cream, leaving a gap round the edges.

Starting at the scored end, lift the edge of the paper under the sponge and use it to help you roll the sponge as firmly as you can. The paper stays outside the roll. It should feel like using a rolling pin inside a bag!

Transfer the rolled up sponge to a serving platter and trim off the ends if you think it needs a neater appearance.

By now the ganache should be thickening as it cools. Whisk it with a balloon whisk or electric mixer until it becomes thick and velvety. Spread over the roulade and mark with a fork. Place in the fridge to set before serving.

Cook's notes

If you are worried about the sponge rising, use self-raising flour instead of plain flour.

The finished roulade keeps for 2-3 days in the fridge if well wrapped.

It can be frozen, though the ganache tends to part company with the sponge on thawing unless very well covered.

Make it a little lighter

Omit the ganache covering and dust with icing sugar to serve.

Variation

Omit the cocoa powder in the sponge and use 4 oz (110 g) of flour instead. Spread the outside of the roulade with good-quality lemon curd and serve with fresh berries. Eat the same day.

Christmas Brandy Butter Tartlets

A festive alternative to mince pies and not a currant in sight.
Makes 12 tartlets

Pastry

5 oz	plain flour	140 g
1 tsp	icing sugar	5 ml
1 tsp	grated orange zest	5 ml
2½ oz	butter, cubed	70 g
	boiled water	

Filling

1½ oz	candied peel	40 g
1½ oz	soft dried apricots	40 g
1½ oz	dried cranberries	40 g
3 tbsp	brandy	45 ml
1½ oz	butter	40 g
1½ oz	light soft brown sugar	40 g
1 tsp	grated orange zest	5 ml
1½ oz	ground almonds	40 g
1	free-range egg, beaten	1
¼ tsp	ground cinnamon	1.25 ml
¼ tsp	grated nutmeg	1.25 ml
¼ tsp	ground allspice	1.25 ml

You will need a 12-hole jam tart tray. Make the pastry according to the method on page 50, adding the icing sugar and orange zest to the flour. Roll it out very thinly and line the wells with pastry circles.

Preheat your oven to 190ºC (180ºC fan).

Chop the candied peel and dried apricots finely, cut the cranberries in half if they are large. Mix the peel and fruit with the brandy in a small bowl.

Cream the butter and sugar with the orange zest until soft. Add the ground almonds, egg and spices, and mix well. Stir in the brandy and fruit mixture.

Divide the filling evenly between the pastry cases. If there are some pastry trimmings over, you can make small stars to top the tartlets.

Bake for about 20 minutes, or until slightly browned and set. Transfer to a wire cooling rack after a few minutes.

Serve warm or cold, dusted with icing sugar if you wish.

Cook's notes

These tartlets are best eaten on the day of making, or soon afterwards, as the brandy flavour fades quite quickly.

Can be frozen, but to revitalise the flavour once thawed, brush with extra brandy and warm through to serve.

Make it a little lighter

Omit the candied peel, increase the weight of apricots and cranberries to 2¼ oz (65 g) each, and reduce the sugar to 1 oz (30 g). Also add an extra 1 tsp (5 ml) of grated orange zest.

Variation

Swap the brandy for dark rum.

Éclairs

Always a winner in our house. Makes about 8 éclairs

Choux pastry

2 oz	butter	55 g
5 fluid oz	water	140 ml
2½ oz	plain flour, sifted	70 g
2	smallish free-range eggs, beaten	2

Filling

10 fluid oz	whipping or double cream	285 ml
¼ tsp	vanilla extract (optional)	1.25 ml

Glaze

3½ oz	dark chocolate	100 g
½ oz	unsalted butter	15 g
2 tbsp	water	30 ml

Preheat your oven to 200ºC (190ºC fan).

Put the butter and water in a pan and bring to a rolling boil over a medium heat. By the time the water boils, the butter should be melted.

Tip in all the flour and beat the mixture vigorously with a wooden spoon until all the flour is incorporated and there are no lumps. Allow the paste to cool to warm.

Beat in the eggs, a little at a time, until you have a smooth shiny mixture that drops slowly from the spoon. You may not need all the egg. Scrape the paste into a disposable piping bag, or a sturdy freezer food bag.

Run a non-stick baking tray under the tap to wet the surface. Snip the end, or a corner, off the bag and pipe well-spaced lines of choux pastry onto the tray – they should be slightly thicker than your thumb and a bit longer than your palm.

Bake for 25-35 minutes, or until the éclairs are a deep golden brown all over. Holding each éclair in a cloth, make small slits in the sides to allow steam to escape. Return the éclairs to the (turned off) oven for 5 minutes. Cool on a wire rack.

When the éclairs are completely cold, whip the cream to peaks, with the vanilla extract if using. Slice open the éclairs along one long side and fill with the cream. *Tip* – use another disposable piping bag, a freezer bag or a long-handled spoon.

Break the chocolate into pieces and put it with the butter and water in a pan. Melt over a low heat, stirring until smooth and shiny.

If you are feeling brave, dip the tops of the filled éclairs into the glaze and leave to set. If not, paint on the glaze with a pastry brush or trickle it over the éclairs with a teaspoon.

Eat within a few hours or the pastry will start to soften.

Cook's notes

Not suitable for freezing.

Make it a little lighter

Make the éclairs smaller!

Variation

Instead of chocolate, top the éclairs with cardamom and lemon icing. Mix 4 oz (115 g) of icing sugar with the crushed seeds from 1-2 cardamom pods, the grated zest of 1 small lemon and enough of its juice to make a pouring consistency. Drizzle the icing over the éclairs and leave to set.

Lemon Tart

A smooth combo of zippy lemon and cream. Makes 1 tart (6-8 slices)

Pastry

8 oz	plain flour	225 g
4 oz	butter	110 g
	boiled water	

Filling

2	large lemons (or 3 small ones)	2
4	large free-range eggs	4
1	egg free-range yolk	1
7 oz	pale golden caster sugar	200 g
5 fluid oz	single cream	140 ml

You will need a 9 inch (22.5 cm) round loose-base flan dish. Make the pastry according to the method on page 50. Roll it out thinly and use it to line the dish, do not trim the edges yet, and let the pastry rest for 30 minutes.

Preheat your oven to 170ºC (160ºC fan). Put a baking sheet into the oven at the same time.

Trim the edges of the pastry case and slide it onto the hot baking sheet. Bake blind for 15 minutes. *Tip* – line the pastry with a sheet of non-stick parchment and then put an 8 inch (20 cm) sandwich tin on top, it's easier than using baking beans.

Take out the flan dish and pastry case, return the baking sheet to the oven and put the dish on a wire rack. Reduce the oven temperature to150ºC (135-140ºC fan).

Grate the zest and squeeze the juice from the lemons and reserve, discarding any pips.

Mix the eggs, extra egg yolk and sugar in a bowl and beat until smooth. Add the cream and beat again. Finally, whisk in the lemon zest and juice.

Remove the baking tray from the oven and set the pastry case, still in its dish, on top. Pour the filling into the pastry case and place the tart gently back in the oven on the tray. *Tip* – spoon in the last bit of filling when the dish is in the oven to prevent spills.

Bake for about 50 minutes or until just set. Leave to cool completely in the dish, ideally still in the (turned off) oven with the door open. This will help prevent cracks in the filling.

When cold, remove the tart carefully from its tin and transfer to a serving plate. *Tip* – leave the loose base on if you prefer. Dredge with icing sugar to serve, if you like.

Cook's notes

Not suitable for freezing. Will keep for a couple of days in the fridge if well covered.

Fresh berries with mint sprigs and crème fraîche make good accompaniments.

Rich Christmas Cake

Start well before Christmas and allow at least three days before you want to bake the cake. Makes 1 cake

6 oz	glacé cherries, halved	170 g
2 oz	candied peel, chopped	55 g
4 oz	dried cranberries	110 g
1¼ lb	mixed dried fruit	570 g
5 fluid oz	medium sherry	140 ml
6 oz	soft butter	170 g
6 oz	dark soft brown sugar	170 g
3	free-range eggs	3
1 oz	ground almonds	30 g
1 tbsp	golden syrup	15 ml
4 oz	plain flour	110 g
2 oz	self-raising flour	55 g
1 tsp	mixed spice	5 ml
	pinch grated nutmeg (optional)	
	pinch ground cloves (optional)	

Put the glacé cherries, candied peel, dried cranberries and mixed dried fruit into an airtight plastic food box. Pour over the sherry, stir the fruit well and cover with the lid. Leave for at least 3 days, shaking the box from time to time, but not taking off the lid.

The cake can take up to 4 hours to bake, so allow yourself enough time. When you are ready to make the cake, preheat your oven to 150ºC (140-145ºC fan).

Butter an 8 inch (20 cm) round deep cake tin and line it with non-stick baking paper, greasing the paper too, or use a good quality ready made non-stick tin liner.

Cream the butter and sugar briefly in a large bowl. Add the eggs, ground almonds and golden syrup and mix well. Sift over the flours and spices and fold everything together. Lastly, stir in all the soaked fruit and any liquid. Make sure the cake mixture is well blended and there are no pockets of flour.

Spoon the mixture into the cake tin and smooth the top. Poke any dried fruit beneath the surface so that it doesn't burn. Give the filled tin one sharp tap on the worktop to dislodge any air voids.

Bake initially for 2 hours, then turn down the oven temperature to 140ºC (130-135ºC fan) and bake for another 1 hour and 15 minutes. Check the cake by inserting a warm metal skewer (or cold bamboo one) into the centre – if it comes out clean, the cake is done. If there are moist crumbs or uncooked mixture still clinging to the skewer, it's not ready and you should keep retesting it every 15 minutes until it's done.

If you think the top of the cake is becoming too brown, lay a piece of foil over the top of the tin but don't tuck it round.

When the cake is cooked, remove it from the oven and allow to cool in the tin. This will take hours, or even overnight if the room is warm.

Once cold, wrap the cake in greaseproof paper and put it in an airtight tin. You can leave it for a few days or a few weeks before icing.

Cook's notes

This rich cake is also wonderful as a celebration bake for a birthday or anniversary, or even for a wedding.

If you have a very sharp knife and a steady hand, this cake should cut into at least 20 slices once decorated.

Make it a little lighter

Difficult – serve very thin slices!

Variation

Add the grated zest of 1 lemon and/or 1 orange with the butter.

Christmas Cake Decorations

Each option is enough to decorate the rich Christmas cake from the previous recipe, or another 8 inch (20 cm) fruit cake. Merry Christmas!

A   Traditional marzipan and icing decoration

For the best result, cover the cake with marzipan one day and add the icing the following day, or after a couple of days.

8 oz	apricot jam	225 g
2 tbsp	water	30 ml
1 lb 8 oz	golden or white marzipan	680 g
	cooled boiled water	
1 lb 10 oz	ready to roll white fondant icing	740 g
	cornflour or icing sugar for rolling	
	food colouring (optional)	

You will need a 10 inch (25 cm) diameter foiled cake board.

Day 1

Place your fruit cake in the centre of the board. *Tip* – for a professional finish, turn the cake upside down to give a flat surface for decorating. Take a piece of string and lay it across the top of the cake and down each side, cut the ends where the cake touches the board. Keep the string.

Boil the apricot jam with the water, and then sieve it to remove pieces of fruit. Brush the cake all over with a thin layer of warm jam. *Tip* – if the jam starts to set in the pan, heat it up slightly.

Roll out the marzipan between two sheets of non-stick baking paper. You need a circle slightly wider than the piece of string.

Lift the marzipan on the rolling pin and drape it over the cake. Using your palms, ease the marzipan over the top of the cake and down the sides, making sure there are no trapped air bubbles. Tuck the marzipan under the edge of the cake and trim around the base.

Ease smooth the surface and trim the base.

Day 2

Brush the marzipan surface of the cake lightly all over with cooled boiled water.

Knead the fondant icing for a couple of minutes make it pliable.

Dust your worktop and rolling pin liberally with cornflour or icing sugar. Roll out the icing to a circle, using the string as a guide. Lift it onto the cake as you did for the marzipan and smooth over the top and sides.

Tuck in the icing at the base and trim to fit. *Tip* – be careful not to cut too close to the cake. Polish the icing using a cake smoother or your (clean) palm.

Colour the offcuts of icing and marzipan if you wish, and use to make decorations for the top of the cake. Leaves, flowers or simple cut-out stars all look good. Stick the decorations to the cake with a dab of cooled boiled water.

Cook's notes

You can make your own almond paste in place of the ready made marzipan if you prefer, though I find homemade a little too soft and grainy to support the icing here, especially if you want to keep the cake for a while after it is decorated.

If I can find it, I like to use a blend of Anthon Berg Raa Marzipan with regular yellow marzipan.

Keep the fondant icing wrapped until you are ready to use it or it will dry out and crack when rolled.

Variation

Royal icing instead of fondant icing.

You will need about 1½ lb (680 g) of Royal icing sugar and 4-6 tbsp of cold boiled water. Mix the icing sugar with half the water and then gradually beat in as much of the remaining water as you need to make a stiffly spreadable shiny paste. *Tip* – an electric mixer will save your arm muscles.

Spread the icing over the marzipanned cake with a palette knife, swirling it to look like drifts of snow. Add decorations of your choice and leave to set.

B   Glazed fruit and nut decoration

An impressive and easy way to decorate your Christmas centrepiece.
Best of all, it can be done at the last moment.

10 oz	thick-cut orange marmalade	285 g
1 tbsp	orange juice or water	15 ml
6 oz	glacé cherries	170 g
4 oz	dried figs, halved	115 g
3 oz	whole Brazil nuts	85 g
3 oz	pecan nut halves	85 g

You will need a 10 inch (25 cm) diameter foiled cake board or decorative serving plate.

Place your fruit cake in the centre of the board or plate, top side up.

Heat the marmalade and orange juice or water in a pan until melted together and beginning to bubble. Remove the pan from the heat and stir in the cherries, figs and nuts.

Brush a little of the juices over the top of your fruit cake. Spoon over the rest of the mixture, and arrange the fruit and nuts to your liking. Leave to set.

Cook's notes

Make sure your marmalade doesn't contain glucose syrup. If it does the topping won't set properly and the fruit could slide off.

If you find marmalade too bitter, try using apricot jam instead. Look for jam containing big pieces of apricot.

You can use all red cherries or a mixture of colours.

Keeps well in an airtight tin in a cool dry place (not the fridge).

Variations

Replace the halved dried figs with halved dates, or whole dried apricots or prunes.

Swap the pecan halves for toasted Marcona almonds.

Index

GF = gluten free

28710013R00057

Printed in Great Britain
by Amazon